"How to reduce life's stress -- or add to it -- by living in the bush"

"Should heating up your bath water be a daily or weekly activity?"

SWEET STEW:
AN ALASKAN TALE

Sweet Stew: An Alaskan Tale

ISBN: 0-9652742-1-7 Library of Congress Number: 96-095425

Published by Aavery Press, W3809 Hwy 14-61, Coon Valley, WI 54623

Printed in the United States of America

The " ^ " is a diacritic and tells how to pronounce the word - it means a gutteral, "tongue in the back of the throat" sound.

*Alutiiq Aleut terms are used throughout the Aleutian story.
*Photo captions by Katie and Anna.
*Narrated by author, Kay.

* *aagusa - lix tunusa - Â: Alutiiq/Aleut) for "true story")*
* *taangadusi Â : bucket*
* *aniqduuda - Â: baby*

ABOUT THE COVER:

This is Erin Katie Rutherford Bartels. We just call our daughter Katie. Katie is sitting and bathing in one of the cooking pots in our industrial kitchen. We live at Cape Sarichef, Unimak Island, the first island of the Aleutian chain, off the southwest coast of Alaska.

Our kitchen and new home is in a deserted coast guard LORAN station. I radio in weather observations for the bush pilots who fly over and out to Dutch Harbor, Unalaska, and my husband, Bob, is the resident bilogist for the Izembeck National Wildlife Refuge here.

Katie has to sit wherever we place her, so here she is — stuck in this pot!

INTRODUCTION:

Alaska called to both Bob and I long ago. When single, I first went to Fairbanks, Alaska during the summer of 1970 to work in a halfway home for Eskimo and Indian Native American girls. A year later, Bob flew to Alaska's Northern waters to collect waterfowl data for his master's thesis in wildlife biology. Several years later, we married and lived for several years in the Midwest, as Iowa is our home state. During this time, I taught school, practiced as a registered nurse, and became pregnant with Katie. Bob worked as a biologist and assistant refuge manager in Kansas. When the opportunity came along, we welcomed the chance to live in a remote Alaskan bush location.

A bush location, generally, means living in an area that cannot be driven to by car, and needs to be flown into. Our first Alaskan bush location was in the Aleutian Islands, so this story's first section consists of photos and stories about our lives from 1979 to 1981 in the Aleutians.

The second set of photos and stories depicts our lives the following two years in Kaktovik, an Eskimo village on Barter Island, which is located in the Beaufort Sea and northeast of the Alaska mainland.

Much heart-warming humor was provided by the antics of our daughter, Katie, and in later years, her younger sister, Anna. These antics kept Bob and I from experiencing too much cabin fever during the wind and loneliness of the Aleutians and the 24-hour darkness and cold of the Arctic.

Katie and Anna probably saw more brown bear, polar bear, sea lions, wolves, fox, caribou, sea birds, otters, whales and tundra wildflowers from their views in the backpacks than Bob and I did.

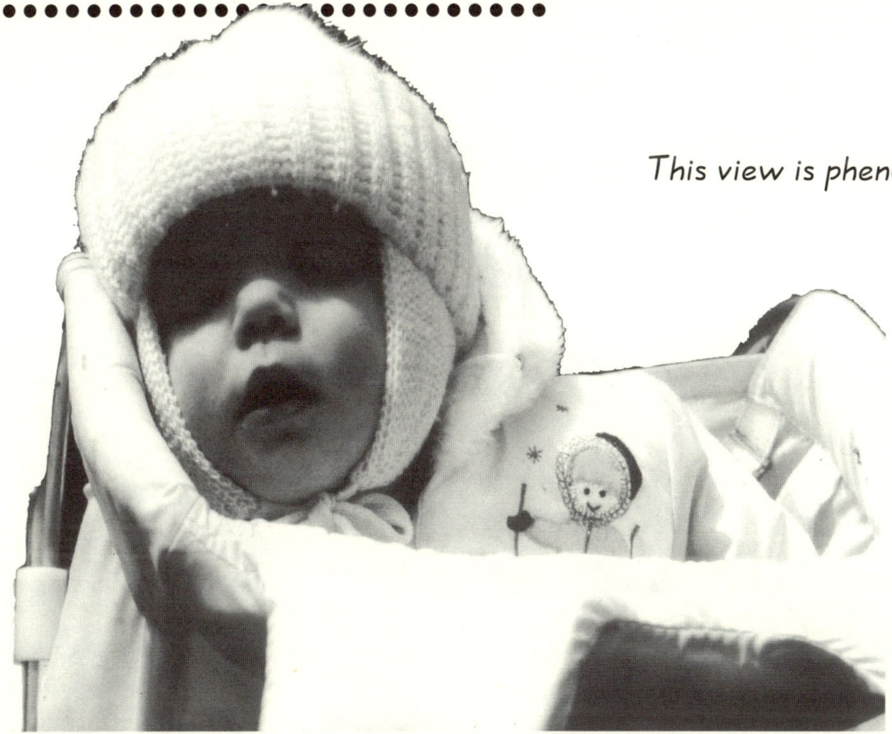

This view is phenomenal!

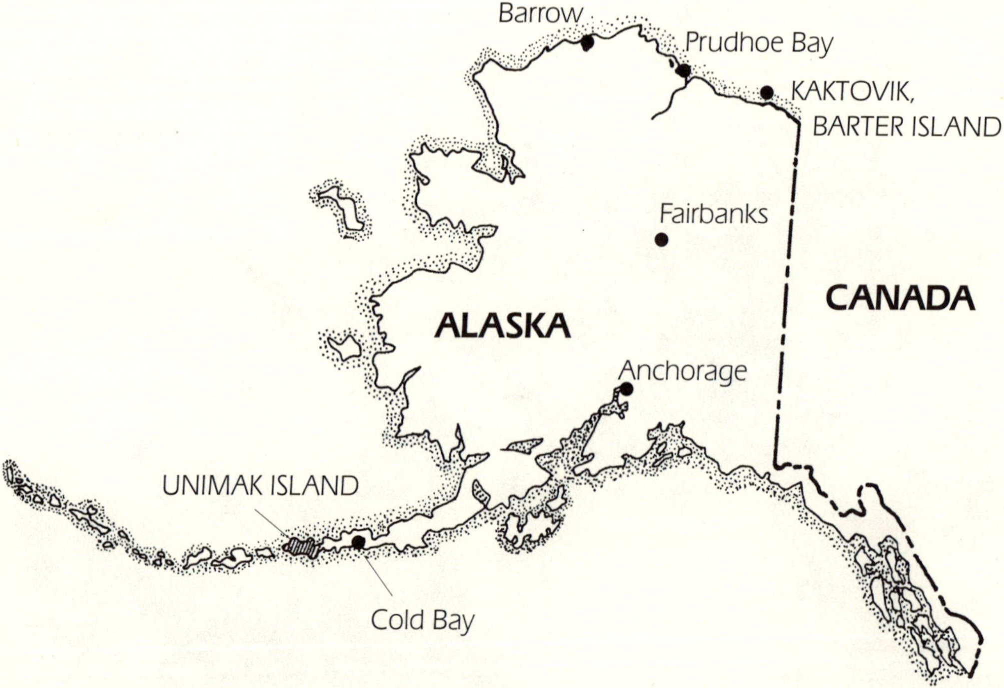
Barrow
Prudhoe Bay
KAKTOVIK,
BARTER ISLAND
Fairbanks
CANADA
ALASKA
Anchorage
UNIMAK ISLAND
Cold Bay

Part I: The Aleutians

The most challenging thing about the Aleutians was, undoubtedly, the weather. Soldiers stationed in the Aleutians during WWII said the weather killed more people in the Aleutians than any warfare. Rain, fog, wind, cold, and wet ... day in and day out.

At this location, we were over 100 miles from the nearest Aleut Indian village of False Pass and 670 air miles southwest of Alaska's major city of Anchorage. "Our" 52-room coast guard building sat at the top of a 200-foot cliff overlooking the Bering Sea. We had a generator for heat and electricity and a reservoir for drinking water. Unimak Island had only a few miles of roads, so our only means of travel to and from town was by airplane.

I arrived at Unimak Island alone and 7 1/2 months pregnant.

I surprised Bob by coming up before our baby was born. He thought I was going to stay in Iowa with my mother until I delivered. Since I previously had a miscarriage, staying in civilization seemed like the wise thing to do. I changed my mind about this, though. First I drove up the Alaska Highway, going 40-45 miles per hour because of the pot holes in the road. For protection, I had pillows under me, behind me, and in front of me. Having been a person who rarely drives 20 miles out of town alone, this was a challenging trip.

The best way to describe the attitude I encountered while driving the highway was "W-h-a-t-e-v-e-r-"! — to use a term frequently used today. I even ran into a few friends from Cherokee, Iowa at a lodge just before the Alaskan border. After nine days of driving, I arrived in Anchorage. The truck was covered with mud. I had an extra tire, but no flats along the way. The only real trouble I had, was when I locked myself out of my truck when I stopped at the side of the road to go to the bathroom in the woods. A gentleman with a neat little bunch of coat hangers got my keys out of the truck for me.

The Alaskan Highway Mud Experience

After parking my car at a friend's in Anchorage, I flew from Anchorage to Cold Bay, a little fishing village down on the Alaska Peninsula. After waiting several days for the foggy weather to clear, I met my first bush pilot, who was to fly me to the island. I had a very large trunk filled with baby clothes — LOTS of baby clothes. I had repeatedly reminded the pilot about this big trunk, emphasizing the need to consider its size, in order to fit it in the small bush plane. Basically, the pilot ignored my request, and just kept packing the plane. When mostly finished with packing, he asked about the trunk. I showed it to him. He then shook his head and exclaimed, "Why didn't you tell me it was so big?! You'll have to wait for another trip. This trunk is too big to fit in this plane now." Then the pilot took one look at me, being very pregnant, and said, " And we're not turning back if you get sick!" Nice guy. Not another word was spoken. As we flew, my view was only of the sea. It looked furiously cold and I thought, "If we crash, I am going to go down in that cold water and this pilot is not going to say one word to me. I'm going to die feeling all

Katie: "I'm inside Mama's tummy, so I can't see much yet."

*piugta, aikuq: dog
*chngatu - lix : sea otter
* sluka - x̂ : sea gull
* aglu - x̂ : orca
* ala - x̂: : whale
* acjima - x̂ : wind

alone." Thus, I started singing, something I do to calm myself. I think the tune was "My Favorite Things". At this point, I didn't care what the pilot thought of me. I just wanted to feel comfortable.

I am resting by the ocean and tired of carrying Katie (photo page 17). She is getting heavy. I'm trying to find a whale or two in the sea and wishing I could swim in all that water that's just too cold. So near and yet, so far. Our dog, Ink, loves having free run of the island. No fences and no neighbors griping about his deposits in their yards. What a life for a dog — his "own" island.

Sometimes, I worried about our living quarters blowing away in the 99-mile-per-hour winds, about the active volcanoes erupting, and about being surrounded by a sea too cold to swim in and too rough to boat in, in case of an emergency. I could imagine the volcanoes erupting, hot lava forcing us to the sea and then not being able to escape! The phrase "sink or swim" didn't hold up in the cold waters of this area.

Eventually, I flew back to Iowa to give birth to Katie. This decision was arrived at because a three or four-week stay in an Anchorage motel waiting to deliver our baby would cost more than a trip to Iowa.

Over twenty thousand grey whales annually migrate from the warm southern waters to the Arctic waters. This meant these whales swam right by our coast. Upon returning to our

Volcanoes, skiing, Mama, Papa, Ink, and ME!"

Aleutian island, we were greeted by eight whale biologists, who were studying this grey whale migration. I was disappointed at first, wanting more private and quiet time with our new little one. But, the researchers were very considerate of us and our space, having been in bush conditions many times before. We ended up having a lovely time celebrating Thanksgiving and Christmas with community meals, volleyball games, and other festivities. I didn't know this then, but we frequently were to house various researchers or bush pilots who became weathered in during their flight.

While playing volleyball in the Coast Guard station's indoor court, we put baby Katie in her car seat and inside a dog carrier in the court. That worked OK until the ball hit her "cage" and scared her! Good grief. What kind of parents are we?

We were now raising Katie, our first-born, with no hospitals, medicines, doctors, strollers, baby-sitters or relatives. My past nursing experience helped, but I then was aware of all the things that could go wrong. I gave Katie all of her immunizations, as the public health service packed them in dry ice and sent them up with us. I worried about Katie reacting to her shots or choking on something. I knew if these things should happen that we could not get help quickly enough to save her.

I had two serious mastitis infections while breast feeding. I waited two weeks for the medicine to arrive by plane. Needless to say, I was uncomfortable. This was our first realization that bush-living required patience and learning to go without what we wanted or needed. I found that standing under hot showers helped a alot.

We are posing for a family photo here (see page 20), the camera is set up on a tripod. You can see that it took us several runs back and forth to get it right. Looks like a herd of caribou just came through. In the background you can see a volcano. We have flown over several active volcanoes. That is something — to see smoke coming out the volcano's top while hovering directly above in a bush plane. It also makes for some rough riding.

Katie doesn't know whether she should eat this thing or study it, as her papa would do. Maybe she's trying to tell us that this stuff is a good source of iodine. The black lava beach includes many things to entice each of us. Katie grabs and tries to eat most anything. In my spare time I make little picture frames out of these shells that have the center washed away.

"Looks like an ancient lava rock to me."

The Aleutians are beautiful and would probably be a resort area if the weather would only cooperate. The beaches are covered with a variety of urchins, mussels, barnacles. The waves are furious, as the Bering Sea meets the Pacific Ocean, and creates very rough waters. Glass fishing floats, Japanese tins, and bottles are washed ashore, as well as whales and sea lions. We now know that sea lions make a definite noise, that sea otters are captivating characters, and that we can see a brown bear approaching quite easily, since the island has no trees.

I think there is nothing really as humbling as the ocean and seeing the creatures in it. I feel very minute compared to the sea, and the whales, especially. Who am I compared to this view of power and beauty?

I also have thoughts like, "Who would know if something happened to us"? Or when hiking alone, I wonder, "What would I do if a bear came up behind me"?

Each afternoon includes a two or three-hour hike with Katie in the front or back pack. So far, I have lost 20 pounds. I think this is from climbing the rock cliffs or the rolling hills on the island. I now know that upward inclines help trememdously when trying to get in shape.

Imagine being surrounded by rolling fields of lupine, and a luscious variety of other knee-deep wildflowers! Not a pesticide or herbicide around. The rain in the Aleutians

Baby and ....BEAR!

provides a climate for full and lush plant growth. My favorites are the lupine, chocolate lilies, monkey flowers, and the abundant supply of berries.

I have a story about hiking and berry picking with my husband, Bob. This is back when I was pregnant with Katie. I was on my hands and knees and thoroughly engrossed with finding every last berry, as berries on the tundra grow spread out

" Love and Lupine"

"Slicker than snot on a brass door knob."

on the ground. Papa came up behind me, growled like a bear and I jumped straight in the air, since I had been forewarned that bears like berries, too. Later, Papa realized that maybe frightening an eight-month pregnant woman on a secluded island was probably not the wisest thing to do.

Berries included lingonberries, strawberries and low-bush cranberries. We made many jars of jam that season which were sent home for Christmas presents. Bob also sent jars of pickled salmon home.

**iqa - x̂ : fish*
**agayuux̂ : : (bird) Cormorant*
**iqya-x̂ : one-holed baidarka, kayak*

Imagine trying to walk on these wet slimy rocks.

I am smiling but Katie is not. Her footing is not as sure.

Katie wants to know what kind of a mother would put on her kid's mittens with the connecting string hanging on the outside (photo pg. 28)?

More about the sea. Barges frequently disappeared from our view, appearing to sink into and under the huge waves. One barge, the only one to actually stop during our two-year stay, brought fuel to our station. We were invited aboard. We hung our coats up and while inspecting the tiny kitchen quarters, I noticed the cook had several sacks of chocolate chips. Our mail and groceries arrived once a month, so luxuries such as chocolate and coca-cola were rationed, and very much coveted. My expression must have given my desire away, for when I put on Papa's old army coat to leave ship, each pocket housed a huge industrial sized sack of chocolate chips! Here we are, way out in the Aleutians, miles from home ... and have I given up my need for chocolate? Not a chance.

I asked the barge hands how they occupied their minds while at sea. One gentleman told me that he watches stars. He could tell me much about the different Northern constellations. I found it fascinating. Since we didn't have trees on the Aleutians, we could see the entire sky; that is, if the sky was not covered up in heavy fog. This view was the same for the barge folks with all of the heavens above them.

Oddly enough, but I admit it — what I frequently missed was junk food. I asked a visiting biologist to bring me a case of coca-cola. He brought me a cheap no-name brand. I was so disappointed. I wanted the real stuff.

We received groceries and mail once a month by plane. Mail/grocery day was chaotic. I wanted to read each letter and take time to soak it in. Bob tore into it all at once and was quickly done with it. All our good news and bad news came at once. I found it to be a very emotional experience. It was kind of like Christmas — all that preparation and packages torn into and opened in minutes!

Food was another thing. We learned to ration it. For example, a half-pound Hershey's chocolate-almond bar had to last an entire month. I would actually eat only one little square every other day. I do remember eating more than my share of other peoples' chocolate. The visiting whale researchers had a huge cache of food stored. One day I went in and ate several squares of their chocolate and I couldn't admit it. So,

"But there's nothin' to do."

*tqagida - x̂ : puffin (horned)

Liam, if you read this book you will now know it was ME!

I also remember hoarding certain items. A visitor drank several cans of our coke. This bothered me, but he probably didn't realize that we would have to wait another month to receive more. I didn't realize back then the meaning of the saying, "What goes around comes around".

We expect Katie to be happy here in this "cage" that Papa made and is so proud of. What does she expect? Her toys are numerous, but I think she'd rather be riding in her backpack (photo pg. 32).

Our coast guard station was not equipped with paraphernalia for babies. Papa made her this play pen consisting of two twin bed mattresses on the floor and a fence surrounding them. We gathered all the toys from assorted relatives and friends, including an Iowan-made monkey doll and a discarded egg carton, and put them and Katie in this cage. We were excited about this invention. Katie was not.

Katie puts on a happy face for this one. After she cleans the sink her next job is the you-know-what. Perhaps she first thought this was a toothbrush. Can you imagine? Katie is "privileged" to have several bathing areas: a plastic oil drum with the top half cut off, a flooded shower stall, kitchen pots and this coast guard dormitory bath sink.

"This is only a part-time job."

Katie says this is not strollering and that she'll have hemmorrhoids before she's two. We have no "Preparation H" with us and the nearest pharmacy is 700 miles away! It's pretty bumpy on the gravel pathways here. We have an air strip about a mile from our building and one gravel road to it. We devised a way to transport Katie by padding an appliance dolly with pillows and strapping Katie into it with an old seat belt, but it's hard to push a dolly on a rock and gravel road.

"Hey, I'm not a refrigerator!"

tanĝaaĝim chumnuga : brown bear

We did national weather observations for the bush pilots and radioed in the information. One of the ways we tested for visibility was to see which volcano or mountain we could see clearly in the distance. During the months of June and July, I reported fog cover too dense for bush pilots to fly in 53 days out of 61. That's a lot of fog. One of our Midwestern friends, Guy, came up to shoot photos and it was a real challenge for him to find a day with sufficient sunshine. Yet, photos taken in the fog yield an eerie, filmy cast to a wildflower or mountain setting.

One of our whale-watching friends, Polly, provided us with a humorous story. Polly is a vegetarian and was frequently eating unusual things, at least from our Midwestern point of view. She was known to take a dry smashed package of seaweed, put it in water, only to have it "come alive" and then be eaten by her. After leaving us, she sent us a care package which included a loofah, which Polly wrote and explained "was the inside of a squash". Knowing that Polly ate unique things, we assumed it was something to eat. After trying to boil and fry it, we gave up and wrote to Polly, "How do you eat this thing?"

We could hear her laughter upon reading her response. "Not to eat," Polly said, "but to use on dry heels and elbows!" We tell this story not to embarrass ourselves, though you may feel it could have possibly been an embarrassing situation, but to point out two facts: 1) One of the perils of living in the "bush" is that we missed out on the latest fads. How were we to know what a loofah was for? We had no TV and our AM/FM radio only played Russian voice and music, and 2) Who was around with whom to be embarrassed ?

Part II: The Arctic

After two years in the Aleutians, we moved to the Arctic for two more years of bush living. Our second home was in Kaktovik, a little Eskimo village off the Northeastern coast of Alaska, and on an island called Barter Island. Kaktovik is an Eskimo name which means "to seine fish".

I taught K - 12 music in the Arctic North Slope Borough School and worked as a substitute village postmistress. Bob was a biologist for the Arctic National Wildlife Refuge, which consists of the northern top one-third of the state of Alaska.

Barter Island is approximately 360 miles from the town of Fairbanks, which is in the interior of the state. The island is somewhat even in latitude and about 40 minutes by air from Prudhoe Bay, where the Alaskan pipeline begins. Farther west is the Eskimo village of Barrow.

We left the fog, wind and rain in the Aleutians for the cold, snow and 24-dark (or 24-hour daylight) of the Arctic. We were now wearing winter parkas rather than Gortex rain suits. It was hard to realize we were on an island, because the entire area was covered with frozen ice and snow for nine months each year. The village population consisted of 150 Eskimos and 15 Caucasians. Kaktovik included a post office, a large public school, a front porch junk food store, several

apun : snow
nutagak : fresh snow, powder
aniu : packed snow
natiguik : snow drift
kaiguglak : rippled surface of snow
auksalak : melting snow
kaaktugvik : Barter Island
nunaakkik : village

* Inupiat Eskimo terms are used throughout this Arctic story.

houses, and an airport. There was also a military dewline sight about three miles away from the village, which meant, compared to our life in the Aleutians, we now had more dependable and frequent transportation and deliveries by air.

Why did I want to live this North Country? I loved winter and winter sports. I also loved the challenge of living in the cold and the wild. I liked the therapy of working hard just to survive. It somehow fulfilled a need that I have in me. My mother says I should have been a pioneer. I have always like to mix cookie dough by hand, to see the flour mix into the other ingredients, etc. This has come in handy, because we made our own bread for over two years — and by hand, with no mixers, Mom!

One of the biologist technicians flew in from his home state of North

Dakota to work a season on Barter Island. As he climbed out of the plane, his expression of "UFFDA!" summed it up quite effectively. All he could see for miles was white. White snow, white sky, white everything — no trees.

I first realized I was pregnant again when we were enroute and moving from the Aleutians to the Arctic, so I visited a doctor while staying over in Fairbanks. Eight-plus months later, my second and last doctor's appointment was three weeks before our baby was due, when we flew into Fairbanks.

We lived in a motel during those weeks in town and Bob worked out of the federal office in Fairbanks. By this time,

A simple
Arctic flight

24-hour darkness had settled in the Arctic and Bob couldn't do much field work up there, anyway.

While sitting — uncomfortably, I might add — in the motel, I actually watched the movie "Cannery Row" (with Nick Nolte and Debra Winger, based on John Steinbeck's novel) on 24-hour HBO thirteen times! Not only was it hard to sleep at this point but we hadn't watched TV for about 2 1/2 years.

Anna Leah Maggie Rutherford Bartels was born on December 17, 1981. Bob says she sounds like a baroness with that string of names.

This next photo (pg. 46) was taken of Anna while she was sleeping on the floor of the airplane. We are in a big cargo plane, one without official seats. Anna is wearing a little bunting made by our new Kaktovik friend, Cindy. Cindy made an insulated "sack" with legs, but no arms. This works well for warmth. The bunting's ruff is made of a beaver pelt.

Anna is snug and secure in it. Katie says Anna sleeps alot — more than she ever did. "That's for sure!" I say.

I am not particularly worried about our health. By now, I am getting used to bush living. I think I am healthier when living in the bush. I do more walking here than I do in the Midwest. I also have fewer conflicts. No one is calling me to work here or work there. I have more time with my babies at home, which I like very much.

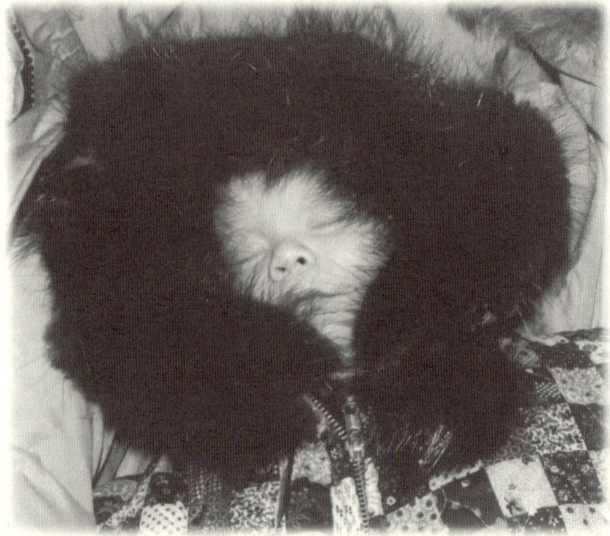

"Sacked out in a beaver ruff"

Besides being dark, the winters here are cold — an understatement. The coldest we saw in Kaktovik was -50 degrees Fahrenheit. We even took a photo of the thermometer this day. Surprisingly, Kaktovik is situated on the coast so the ocean winds actually warmed our temperatures, for Alaska's interior areas frequently get much colder than -50.

* *paipiivak* : *baby*
**paluktak* : *beaver*

Sometimes, the cold and darkness got to us, even though we didn't like to admit that it did. Studies said it is the darkness that gets to people — for then cabin fever sets in. I think we made big of small happenings, irritating ones, which was a sign of cabin fever or light deprivation.

I think, too, I learned what it was like to be the minority in a small village. Sometimes I got lonely. I think, eventually, especially if we had stayed there a long time, I would have gotten homesick.

This was NOT a simple picnic. You know in retrospect, how we tend to remember the good things? I am more realistic now and remember how long it took to simply dress for this little social experience. We were bundled up to go on a winter picnic with our Kaktovik friends, Charlie and Cindy. Anna is that obscure bundle

"A simple winter picnic... or, are we having fun yet?"

hidden behind and inside my parka. Katie is standing in front of Papa and if you look closely, you will see that she is somewhat stiff from the cold. We are smiling, but I have just complained incessantly about my frozen feet, even though I am wearing bunny boots, the warmest possible Arctic boots. Papa's mustache is totally iced over. I suppose we had to put on a good, brave show for our friends. If I remember right, this picnic was THEIR idea.

* *tanik*: *white person*

Charlie was one of the village policepersons. Cindy was the unofficial village nurse, now that people knew she was a nurse.

"Snow Blindness"

It is amazing that Katie is smiling in this whiteout. It's also amazing that we could even get a clear photo. Katie is wearing her first real winter parka. The ruff is wolverine fur and is supposedly the best fur for the prevention of freeze-up around her face. Back when Katie was very small, I carried her deep

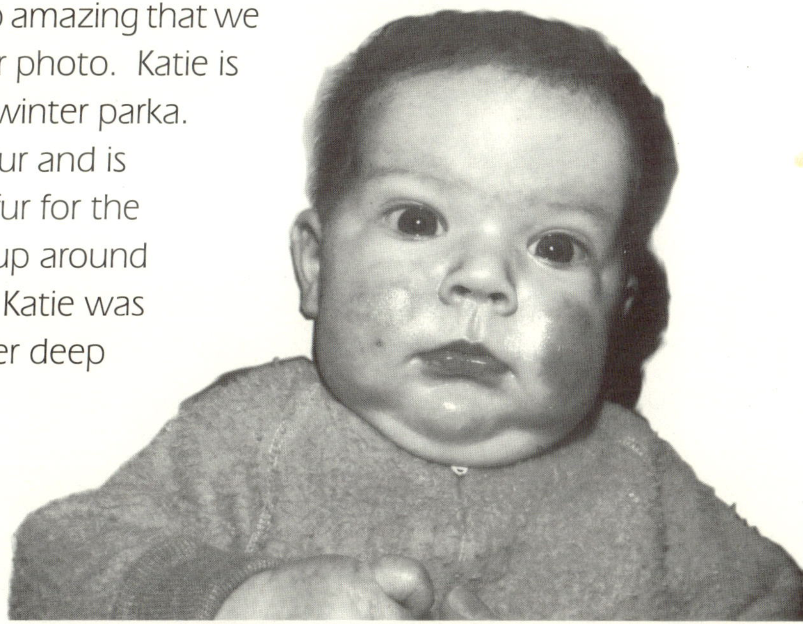

Do you think my cheeks will stay this way?

in the front of my parka, and somehow her cheeks still became frostbitten. This was the point at which I decided that animal fur is a necessity in the Arctic and not just a luxury.

*kuvyugagniksuk : is white out
*amaakuk : carry baby on back
*ukpik : snowy owl

The rest of Katie's parka is made of tuscany lamb's wool which has been sewn together with dental floss, to keep the needle holes from tearing. The fur of the body of the parka is turned inside and against Katie's skin for warmth. The cover, a "kuspuk", is made of a cotton calico fabric. Bright Hawaiian prints are often used for these covers. I think the purpose of these bright parka cover colors is to create a fun change from all the white of winter. Girls traditionally have little ruffles on the bottom skirt of their parkas. Boys have pockets in the

front of their parkas. Eskimo women have parkas made with an additional hump cut out on their upper backs. This makes room for babies to ride on their mother's backs inside the parka.

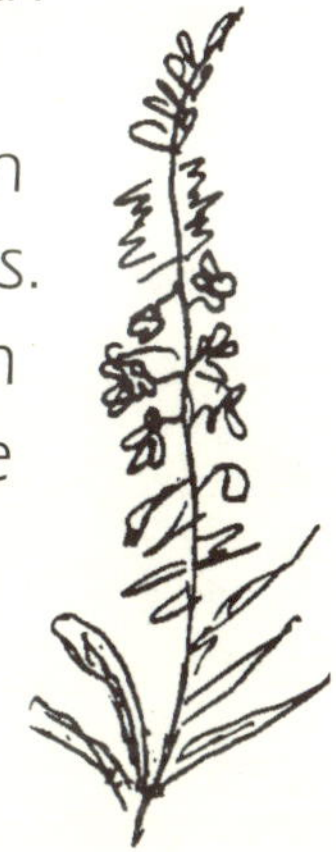

Anna conveys to me that this Arctic "dressing up" is wearing her out. I dress Anna in mukluks (fur boots), snowpants, and these mummy parkas! Then I dress up Katie and myself. After all of this, we are all very hot and rather irritable. And what for? A simple three-block walk to the post office. Anna usually gets pulled in a sled up and down the snow hills, as it is too hard for me to carry her with all this stuff on.

"Life on the tundra isn't all it's cracked up to be."

*alappuu : is cold

Annie, an Eskimo woman, made this parka for Katie. It cost us $70.00, in 1980. The little hand openings were sewn over with tuscany fur for warmth. The parka had no zipper, which kept the wind from blowing in. Katie needed help getting this parka on. She stood with her arms straight down and then I slipped the parka on over her body. Katie then slid her arms up and through the arms of the coat. At the end of a preschool day, the teacher lined up the students and helped them slip into their individual parkas. Quite a process.

Anna's parka had a double ruff. I sewed on an additional lighter colored wolf ruff. This double thickness helped for warmth especially when we pulled the ruffs forward to make a wind tunnel in front of her face.

One of my chief free-time activities in the bush was sewing. I cut up sheets to use for quilt backings and old woolen skirts to make wool pants

for my daughters. I used flannel material for many of my girls' outfits. It fit the bill for warmth and softness. I made mukluks for the girls out of lambswool and attempted a few parkas.

**atigi : pull-over parka*
**atikttuk : parka cover*

Under subsistence provisions, the Eskimos in Kaktovik are allowed to harvest three whales per fall season. A village whaling festival,

"Blubber...better than a pacifier."

called Nalukatuk, is held on the Fourth of July. Anna is wearing her new parka and chewing on a big piece of muktuk (whale meat & blubber). Her parka will smell like whale for a long time. Anna likes this whale meat so much that an Eskimo gentleman asked if he could take her picture. He laughed and exclaimed, "Anna needs to stay here a long, long time!"

Visitors to Kaktovik (or other bush villages) frequently took photos of the Eskimos. As residents of the village we rarely took photos, but if we did, we asked permission first. For this reason, it was a real treat for Eskimos to ask us (as taniks, or "white persons") if they could take photos of us.

I was pregnant the first year that I tried eating raw whale and blubber. I had to walk around to the other side of the tent and spit it out. The second year, though, I was not pregnant, and I handled it quite well.

The whale harvest

Bob did not want to try it, as his biologist's fear of parasites kept him away.

* *tuttu* : caribou
* *akkaa* : smells bad
* *uminmak* : musk ox

What a day it is when a whale is brought in! Children are let out of school and everyone gathers at the beach. The elders sit on a mattress sharpening the knives. The 52-foot blue whale is pulled onto shore with two bulldozers. The whale's flipper is the delicacy. The meat is left on the tundra to freeze until the summer festival when the whale meat is passed out to all. Frozen and raw is the favorite way to eat the whale and blubber.

For the celebration Eskimo blanket toss, the Eskimos stretched a blanket of walrus skins — which does not stretch and give like a trampoline — I found out! In the old days, the blanket toss was used to get up high and look out into the waters to search for whale. Also, in the past, Eskimos and ropes pulled the whale onto the beach and not bulldozers!

* *nalukatak* : blanket toss
* *aguaktak* : killed a whale
* *agvik* : bowhead whale
* *akikkak* : fluke
* *tuttuvak* : moose

Why is it that this happens? Maybe it's because it takes us so darn long to get dressed for this cold weather in the first place.

"But I have to go to the bathroom."

"Potty training on a three-pound coffee can."

Katie's potty chair is a three-pound coffee can with a hole cut in the plastic lid. We want to patent this idea. The same thing can be used when camping in the tent, as well.

Most homes in the Arctic had "honey buckets". These unique toilets consisted of buckets with toilet lids attached to the tops for careful sitting upon. The

* *ukpik : willow*

buckets were lined with plastic bags. Heaven help the guests who put their cigarettes out in the honey buckets! When full, the bags were twisty-tied and carried to a waiting discarded diesel fuel barrel outside. This presented no problem in the winter, as the barrel contents froze, but it was odiferously evident when spring thaw came around. Time to dump the barrels.

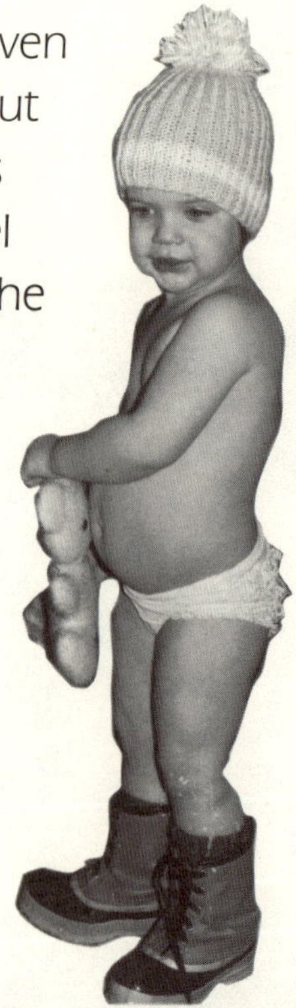

"Profile of Prosperity"

or

"Maybe a little less blubber?"

or

It's waist-deep out here...and my sorrels don't even reach my knees!

Katie is finally fitting into her sorrel boots. Like Papa says, "She'll wear 'em out before they fit her! I am always buying things that the girls have much room to grow into.

The bare essentials. Spring break up is when all the snow melts in the Arctic. It means a summer of 3-feet deep puddles. It is not uncommon for little ones to drown, as not too many Kaktovik children know how to swim. This also presents another thing for me to worry

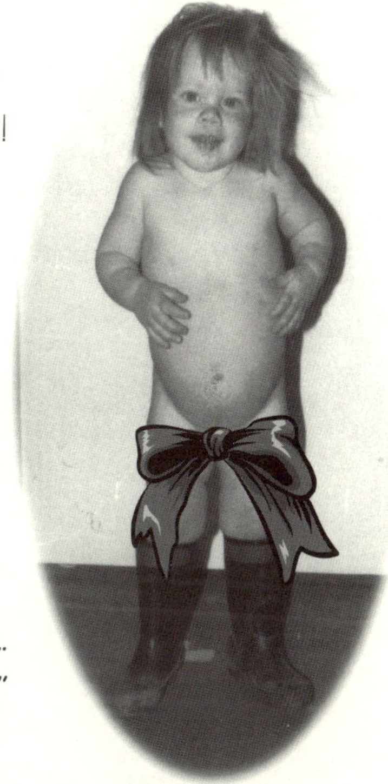

"The sun will come out tomorrow..
Bet your bottom dollar....."

**ukalliurak : hare*

"A rest break on Main."

about. I cannot let Katie and Anna play outdoors in a fenced in back yard. No fences and a yard filled with deep water.

Most houses in Kaktovik were built on stilts. This helped with the snow and water problems — too much snow to get through in the winter and too much water to get through in the summer. It seemed better to walk above the elements than through them. There were no sidewalks, so none to shovel. No lawns of grass to mow, either. At spring break up time, pieces of plywood were spread from house-to-house to walk on.

Uff-da!

The snow in the Arctic is so dry it is very easy to simply sit down and slide down a hill. The blue-white snow is blown into varying shapes which are so stiff they are hard to walk on or ski across. Snow shoes are needed.

**aniiksuaktuk : play outdoors*

"No need for sleds...

or

"Mama's pregnant... honest!"

(With Anna's smile, she could probably talk someone into a free Big Mac.)

"How far to the nearest fast food?"

In the far distant background of this photo you can see an old diesel fuel barrel. The Arctic is strewn with these, left from the pipeline days.

There are miles of tundra in the

Arctic. This photo was taken in the spring, when the snow is melting fast. Our back yard had a view to the South and we could see the Brooks Mountain Range on a clear day. Not a single tree for hundreds of miles.

*akargik : willow ptarmigan

Transportation in the village was by three-wheeler in the summertime and by snowmachine (mobile) in the winter. On the snowmachine, Katie sat bundled up in her parka and faced backwards snuggled into Papa's front. This way the wind didn't freeze her tender face. Anna wouldn't ride on the snowmachine — too noisy — she said it hurts her ears.

"Arctic sunbathing..."

How a little sun improves an Arctic summer! It is wonderful to have no coats on. Katie may get a tan. Anna is still looking for a Big Mac...under the snow, perhaps?

Katie and her friends are sitting on what is our driveway—two adjoining pieces of plywood. Our garage is small and built for snowmachines only, not cars or trucks. Once we drive our snowmachines into the garage, we then have to lift and turn them around so we can drive them out. Not a small task for me. They are heavy machines. We also had a little swing hanging in the garage for the girls. There are no trees in the Arctic to hang a swing on.

Summer temperatures averaged about 45 degrees Fahrenheit. We just needed a light jacket or sweater, unless the wind came up. Mosquitoes were almost nonexistent there because of the sea winds. However, when hiking inland, we were reminded that mosquitoes do, very much, exist.

Can you believe this?

"But my bangs are greasy!"

Maybe Anna's just testing the temperature of the water (pg.72). Or perhaps there just isn't enough room for the rest of her! This is our bathtub.

We have water by gravity flow in our house. The village truck delivers water and pumps it up to our tank upstairs. We have only cold water, so each bucket for the bath has to be heated. We also have a shower stall with a barrel to fill and hang above. Handy idea, but once it is full, it is too heavy for me to lift, so we girls stick to the tub baths. Papa manages a shower each AM. In fact, he gets sick when flying in small planes unless he has his AM shower!

* *kasigiak : spotted harbor seal*

All this heating up of water for baths and laundry sounds like a lot of physical work, but I really liked it. It was, somehow, very therapeutic. Back to the pioneer spirit. Now and then our propane line froze up and Papa had to go out and thaw it.

This demonstrates one of my tricks. It is worth watching, and perhaps, even charging admission. It's possible to fit myself in this tub at eight months pregnant. I have to stand and cross my legs first and gently ease down into a sitting position. My only other original trick is to swim feet first on my back, but waters here are too cold for that, and this tub isn't big enough!

**kuppikutak : fireweed*

"A good book is hard to put down."
(Sacajawea, one of my favorites.)

(Actually, Katie and her cat do not know what their papa would do without them.)

Eventually, we got a larger tub, which of course, became our community bath, cat included. Some of us had to wait longer for our turn than others.

"Cat in a tin tub."

* *ovvaktik* : *bathes*

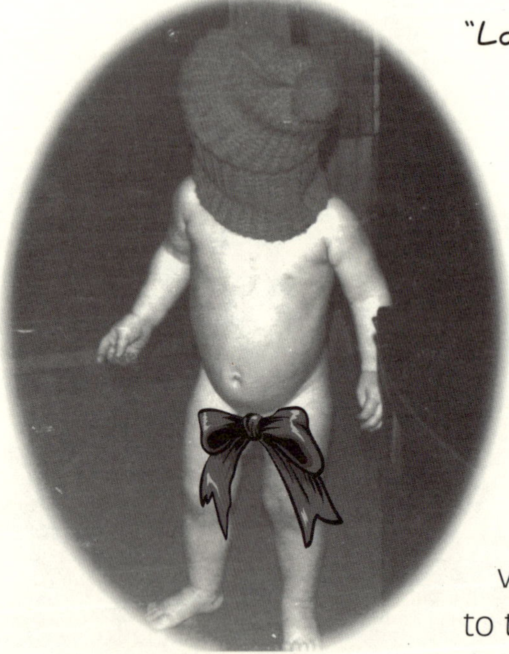

"Land of the Midnight Sun."

(And they told me the sun would shine 24 hours per day up here.)

Anna is exploring in our home. Our federal government house is large and new. It is situated on the outside edge of the village. Our painted wooden floors allow for muddy and snowy boots. Since we have no hot water heater or plumbing, the house will not freeze up when we leave and fly to town.

*kamik : mukluk, boot

One evening the chimney for our fuel oil heater froze up and the fumes came back inside. At this time I was alone with the girls as Bob was in Fairbanks for a few weeks. At three AM I felt kind of "airey" and sort of uneasy. I hiked the three of us down to our friend Charlie's house. Waking Charlie up was one of my major accomplishments in life. He is a very deep sleeper. Once awake, Charlie came up and shot the ice off the chimney — a clever trick, in the cold and the dark.

We flew into Fairbanks about once every six months, and our first activity once there was to luxuriate in a long, deep bath with an unlimited supply of very hot water. A two-hour bath was not uncommon.

Transportation to and from town was by plane. Driving to Kaktovik was not possible, as there were no roads. When I flew with Katie and

Anna, I sat in between them with my arms wrapped around each of them and holding plastic bags under their mouths. Only a mother could love such adventure.

"Is that the meter man?"

or

"Is that a polar bear?

(Cold on the outside,
not bad on the inside.)

* *nanuk : polar bear*

Polar bears were indeed common on our island. After a bowhead whale was harvested on the beach, the whale bones were left and polar bears came onto the beach to get the bones. We would then have quite a bit of excitement. Bob tried to fly the bones out by helicopter and drop them into the sea to keep the bears from coming right into the village.

I told Bob I would move anywhere as long as I could have a piano. The piano moving presents another story. First, our piano was flown in by bush plane. To get it across town and up to our house, it was laid on its back and onto a sled. Then a snowmachine pulled the sled. I stayed in the house and watched. After years of moving several pianos, I know

when disappearing is the best way of helping. Whenever we moved, Bob would ask me under his breath, "Why don't you play the harmonica?"

"Bottoms and windows."

Everyone needs a place to call their own and Katie has found her place (pg. 80). Our home has twelve inches of insulation in the walls so we have twelve-inch window ledges. Katie doesn't miss much.

The typical one or two-room Arctic home had a lot of stuff out in the open. Nails held pajamas and towels and open shelves were filled with supplies. Pans hung from the ceiling and boots set just about anywhere. The diaper changing table was in the kitchen. We had a tiny washing machine that could wash two pair of men's jeans at one time. A separate compartment spun the water out of them and then they were line-dried. We were lucky, as many villagers had no washing machines, at all. In fact, one

Kaktovik resident put on a clean pair of jeans the first of each month and wore the same until she changed to a new clean pair the first of the next month.

"We hardly have a minute to ourselves."

Katie: Mama, can I have puppies in my tummy?

Dogs and puppies were very common in the village. We inherited this dog who later had two puppies. Katie named them "Here" and "There". We sent out birth announcements with paw prints and birth weights included. Papa weighed the puppies with his fish scale (our next book will be entitled Unique and Varied Entertainment in the Arctic). Deciding who got which puppy was not hard, as Katie did not want the wrinkled (curly) one.

> * *kimmiagruk* : puppy
> * *pisukkaak* : fox

Rabid fox and dogs were a problem in the Arctic. Bob had to be very careful of cuts and contamination when cleaning a fox hide for a parka ruff.

To trap a fox, we dug a hole in the snow and put some whale meat and a trap in the hole. We covered the meat and trap with a rectangular, flat piece of snow that we cut out of the hard snow. We shaved this flat piece of snow with a long knife until it was very thin. When stepped upon, it broke through easily. This was how igloos could be

" Tie this to a sled dog, will you?"
(For heaven's sake, you don't expect me to get out and pull it myself, do you?)

built for temporary shelter. The dry snow could simply be cut into squares and piled up.

Anna's new little tricycle is nearby but she chooses the cardboard box for us to pull her around in.

Speaking of pulling, few Kaktovik Eskimos have teams of sled dogs any more, at least not in this village. They say it is too much work to feed them. Now they have snowmachines.

* *uniat* : sled

* *kinmik* : dog

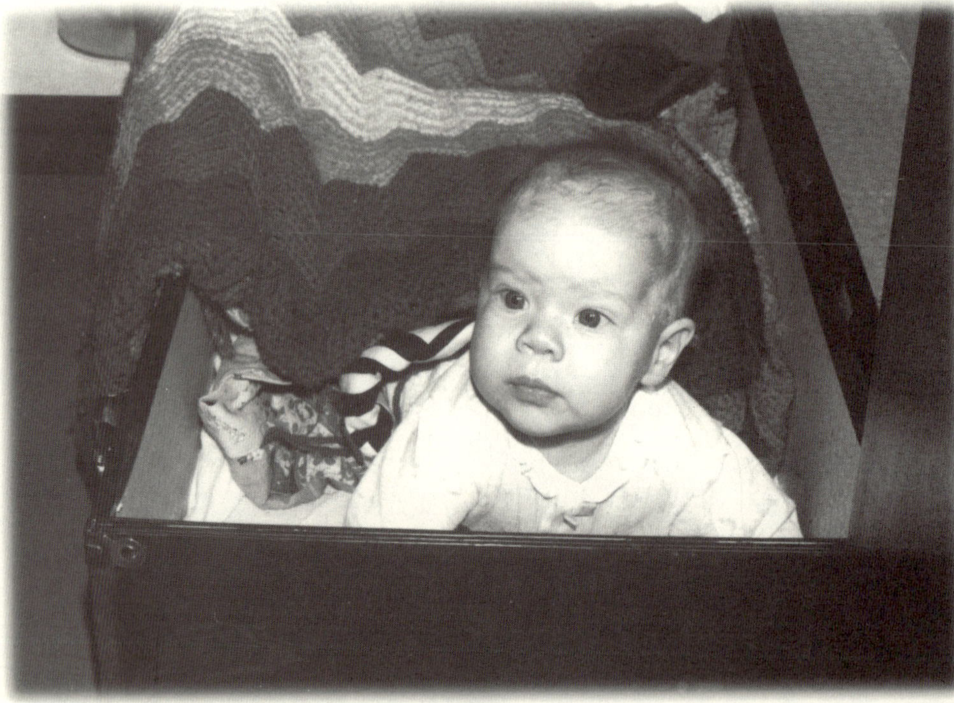

"But I don't want to go to boarding school."
(How could a kid who sleeps in a trunk be expected to even go to school?)

* *pikpaksriruk* : loves, precious

Anna is three months old and is sleeping in her off-the-kitchen-nap-time bed, a trunk with the lid tied onto the dishtowel rack — we'd hate to have the lid fall down. Anna has her very own hand-made crib in the walk-in closet upstairs, as well. That is really her bedroom.

"In your Easter parka...."

**amaguk : wolf*

I say, "A photo is worth many words".

Katie says, "I will never forgive you for this one".

An Arctic style show with Katie modeling her summer parka, which we bought at a Kaktovik yard sale. It is a zippered affair with a wolf ruff.

EPILOGUE:

I write this now in 1997. I have known that I would one day piece these photos and stories together and share them with family and friends. My girls, Katie and Anna are now, respectively, 17 and 15 years old.

Presently, the girls and I have just moved from another year spent in Fairbanks, Alaska. We are now living back in the Midwest, near LaCrosse, Wisconsin.

Not all things go as planned. Bob and I are no longer married. Bob has recently moved back to Alaska. Our experiences in the Alaskan bush taught us many values that we previously believed in, but even more so now. The values of simplicity, solid friendships, true adventure, realness and how to dress for the weather stay with us.

Many times, now, I miss the simplicity and challenge we had in Alaska. Sometimes, I have a hard time finding friends who like basic ideas and basic homes. It's hard to find friends that want to walk instead of ride, or that want to go out for a walk in a blizzard. Now, I fear I may get too soft.

When I first started dating, after becoming single again, I sometimes found men friends who were more interested in their new car than a camping weekend. Or someone who wanted to fly to Tucson to golf (with a golf cart even!) rather than spend an evening baking bread. Imagine!

I try to pass on simple values in my work as a counselor. Frequently, I encourage clients to walk and talk, rather than just talk, or to simply enjoy the elements of nature, as therapy. Or to get back to the basics of making gifts, or bread or jam. I also have worked to become a Type B person rather than a Type A.

I think our girls know the values of simplicity. For the most part, they do not seem to need many of the latest clothes or too much of "just stuff". I hope this sticks.

I wish my girls, Katie and Anna, joy in their adventures of realness, and I hope their experiences are filled with many humorous incidents. I thank them for being excellent companions in life.

I thank Bill for encouraging me to write for pure fun.

The photos in this book are by both Bob Bartels and Kay Rutherford.

The sketches are by Kay, Katie and Anna.

We dedicate this book to Babushka and her many adventures.

William R. Pfisterer, author of Kaiiroondak: Behind the Willows, the Alaskan book depicting the oral history of the life and terms of Richard Marten, says: Kate Rutherford has taken daily child rearing events and showed them in uniquely Alaskan living situations. Her vignettes reminds us that conveniences so often taken for granted are, in fact, luxuries in other geographic settings. I had a great time reading and laughing over everyday occurrences in this young family's adventure.

From Dr. John Littrell, ED.D., author of Brief Counseling in Action: Choices, Changes & Cheers: I've always thought of Kate (Kay) as a "woman of the frontier". This story of her family's Alaskan experiences confirms this. I feel privileged to be coming along on her journey.

References:

Aleut Dictionary: Unangam Tunudgusil: compiled by Knut Bergland, Alaska Native Language Center, University of Alaska, Fairbanks, Alaska, 1994.

Inupiat Eskimo Dictionary, by Donald Webster & Wilfried Zibell, Alaska Rural School Project, Department of Education, University of Alaska, College Alaska, 1970, Summer Institute of Linguistics, Inc.

If you would like a copy of this book for yourself or would like to order it for a special friend, it is $9.95 (postage is already included).

To order Kay Rutherford's first book, "And, I Don't Mean Christmas!", A Children's Photo Journal, it is $5.95 (postage is already included).

Please make check out and send to:

Aavery Counseling and Press
W3809 Hwy 14/61
Coon Valley, WI 54623
(608) 452-3811

Back Page photo and author note:

Author, Kay Rutherford, and daughters, Anna and Katie, pose for their family Christmas photo in the Arctic. This fascinating true story describes their many adventures while living in Alaska's Aleutian Islands and far North "bush" country. Humorous incidents and photos make their story real for each of us.